There

Marie Redekop.

There

ROY MIKI

VANCOUVER I NEW STAR BOOKS I 2006

NEW STAR BOOKS LTD.

107 – 3477 Commercial Street, Vancouver, BC V5N 4E8   CANADA
1574 Gulf Road, #1517, Point Roberts, WA 98281   USA
www.NewStarBooks.com   *info@NewStarBooks.com*

Publication of this work is made possible by the support of the bpNichol Memorial Fund, the Government of Canada through the Canada Council and the Department of Canadian Heritage Book Publishing Industry Development Program, and the Province of British Columbia through the British Columbia Arts Council and the Book Publishing Tax Credit.

Cover by Mutasis.com
Printed and bound in Canada by Gauvin Press
First printing, November 2006

LIBRARY AND ARCHIVES CANADA
CATALOGUING IN PUBLICATION

Miki, Roy
    There / Roy Miki.

Poems.
ISBN 1-55420-026-1

    I. Title.
PS8576.I32T44 2006   C811'.54   C2006-903036-7

for my friends

About

Sure it sounds like a cliché
in the morning as the mirror

Rinses the residue of sleep

The tap runs on program
And hands conjure her face

Slavishly giving one cause
to pause in the long chain

The cliché is the uninvited
resonance of blue waves

Sink in the subaltern

Should one pause long
enough for winds to change

The chain of emery is the cliché
of haphazard sand dunes

When in the sleeper's eye
the ocean swells in the orbit

Stuck in the floater that conceals
this replay of powdered cheeks

So here's another one
already forms the mirror

As if a silent witness were to say

We have no recollection of the incoming tide

Photo by Glenn Baglo/*Vancouver Sun*, courtesy Pacific Newspaper Group.

The Young Kid

The moment he laid eyes on the scene he thought he could recognize its import. The minimalism of the gestures – the eyes and hands, of course, but the cocooning effects too – offered stories that seemed to call for reckoning.

In the old sense?

That was subjective musing on his part. In this more material instance the pattern of relationships – mobilized with such acumen in the postwar years, those nestled in memory as the cradle of possibility – had been translated into a mediated phenomenon now dubbed the "reinscription."

Signing one's own name, despite the soft hued nomenclature adopted by the white-collar gatekeepers, could stand in as the tell tale aura that the nation – yes, the nation – had entered, as if momentously, a state of desire for a human face.

The more explicitly complicit social archives aside, it is the interior of that era with which the photo is fortunately – but is "aligned" the word he wants? He couldn't say for certain. Except that the face posited itself between the pillars of a "support system" and what can only be described as "the uncanny."

The tension, of course, always depended on the provisional identity formation of the young kid in question. In other words, is "he" a figure of destiny or chance?

As he gazes at the hand of the man who incarnates the historical process, holding in his hands the artifact as proof, he does not look at the authorial centre who is caught in this reflection of his power and cannot re-articulate the gaze – which is the nation. This event may be construed, but only tentatively, as the birth of the multicultural.

Look again closely at the conjunction of all the bodies held in place by the image of the image. The hand signing, inscribing his name as the extension of the frame, produces a social relationship. He thought of a photographic inset of the future yet to be – yet to be because the nation, in a symbolic twist, here writes its story on the virile poster and not in his memory.

So when he was a kid, or no, when he was that kid, he couldn't decipher the lingo of his own visibility. He thought he had lost his vocabulary for at least three decades. But then, in a period of idleness, the kind made available in a found image that returns the time of history, he saw himself in the absences necessary to the surge of the very gestures so apparently captured.

It was as if the slippages had yielded a prescience in which the nation had appeared as his double. As a kid, the technique had been lacking. Only an inkling had formed on the tip of his tongue, some hesitancy that had no name, more undertone than an event to be commemorated.

For the time being, at least, he could ride the crest of the not yet, waiting for the arrival of the photographer.

The Fronds on Galiano

There is the word paranoia
that is or isn't all that poetic
in a poem that is

There is the question
of intent or the wholesale
importation of foreign elements

i had arisen to the sounds
as if they had beckoned me
to pronounce this allegiance

outside the ken of readable
fences or the double intake
that resembles a contractual

'i' never more than its speech
imprints on the way to the shore
line in search of displaced rocks

At which point it seeped in
that originary incline in its way
hoaxed the paths before me

coaxed that other word 'property'
into the lexicon of the sauntering
towards the oceanic swells

in what was let's be clear here
the instance of heat on a summer
island road along the dwellings

with their tended gardens
that formed the barrier between
voice and sea and dare i say it

me

The barbed wire fence posts
the sign no hunting or trespassing

"The natives don't want you
to know where the path is"

The clue is in the
plastic red ribbons

two of them hanging
on a nondescript branch

"The only one that looks private to me"

His body signs say it all
say it all it all comes back

in the tranquil bay
the mid-afternoon
sun running on time

"This is not a place to be"

For evidence there are the shades of the emergent figure
a notebook in hand drifting over to the log around which
cluster the multitude of rocks (no two alike

For evidence there was the open road to the beach
there was the open door of the cottage with the welcome sign
the sign of come on in (the prompter button pushed but held back

For evidence there is the gesturing figure superimposed
on that dream of entering the room full of voices
unannounced they speak of compact sketches

"The whole shoreline is public"

"Hope you don't think i'm being obnoxious"

The ferry's roar slices
the ledge of red rock formations

They call them truant sparks
or the haunt of enclosures

the burden of stones
cushioning the sandals

Enter then the garter snake
squiggling (struggling?
out of peripheral view

Local

Late morning Saturday
head north on Highway 6
towards Owen Sound

Patches of black earth mark
the snow covered fields

the flat landscape
punctuated by squat and sturdy
brick farm houses

the skeletal birches look
opulent as the Nissan Pathfinder
(rented of course) enters the time zones

Daphne late last night as we
recalled bp's spiritual drives
saying she'd never thought of
herself living to this time
both of us born in 42

across history the patterns
of departures

Even this line in the forgetting
as the line dividing the cars comes
and goes
even as it becomes visible

Even this urge to write down
what's lost in the debris

as soon as the car pauses in the driveway
as soon as the laptop takes to warm up
its insides already in the winter landscape

Wonder what lines would appear
had i emerged on the main street
of a town called Durham

Head south on Highway 6
out of Owen Sound

through Dornoch
over the River Styx

the country music station
"I'll pour out my soul until it's
empty, empty"

pull into Durham
and think of returning
two decades hence

the buildings unchanged
but renewed with recent coats of paint
the family house still among the birches

Hunger for home as the Nissan purrs
cruising down Galafraxa the Riverside
Restaurant (an old hangout) then left on Douglas
and points beyond

To the right the rolling hills
the sun hangs low under the lifting clouds

grey in the horizon

sheets of snow the mind slowed in
the glittering light through the windshield

on the left above the near full moon
in the fading blue sky

Nowhere to stop

Do Wonder

Do instants
Affect or effect?

The protocol
Calls for briefing

The time scheme
Falls on command

The brow beats
The chest harbours

Estimation gathers
Out to the tail gate

Howls of discontent
Meet the airwaves

Sagacity doubles
As city saga

Fine tunes
Like rustling

Neko's Refrain

for Baco

1

He awoke in the sultry overtones of an almost vertiginous archive. Aghast at the subdued purr emanating from what must have been, at least according to his sense, a kitchen door. Outside on the back porch were some disseminated yet stumbling provocations that shuffled this way and that. He could with little effort make out minimalist sounds, like ah and ba and co, but the language they were ensconced in served to escape him. At least this was the impression left in the margin of the document. His breath held for the moment the intake of all the figures who convalesced in what could be read as the domestic scene of exchange. Even the trail of neko heralded an ongoing testimonial. There and there in the basket of prints the currents rose and infiltrated the camera obscura in her dissolving hands.

2

On the perimeter
against the walls

uneven waves
beckoning neko

as unsettled lips
press to single

strands of stray
hair fallen fallow

In the awakening
folds of furoshiki

detritus specks for
hungry canaries

Lean over awkward
employment sighs

the reticent scratches
on mine walls   permeable

Is it then this black
line that hangs in

the balance wrapt
in the water's prop

again exposed as its
S cuts across *wishes* .

scrambles . unravels
. *water* . *plants* .

3

We is affiliated in the portable mobile
We is detailed in its curvilinear shades
We is assembled in its making belief
We is carried in its resonant hormones
We is able to encode the salty taste
We is the ulterior motive of definition
We is the accumulation of motes
We is solvent in the memory banks
We wants to want the encompassing garments
        The many in the one
The one that is the yellow bird
The one perched on the branch
The weeping voices in the letters
        Apace in their outstretched arms

Even then

IMAGE ON P. 12: *MIYOSHI a taste that lingers unfinished in the mouth (the Pool)*, 2000, by Baco Ohama, photographed by James D. Brown. ABOVE: *MIYOSHI a taste that lingers unfinished in the mouth* (#9 from the postcard project of gathering and dispersal), 2000–2004, by Baco Ohama, photographed by James D. Brown.

If It's Not Asian It Can't Be Good

> *The Oriental immigration problem is one of vital*
> *importance to Canada, not only because of any racial*
> *pride or sentiment that may exist, but because the*
> *problem as to which is to be the dominating race on*
> *the North Pacific Coast of this continent, Oriental or*
> *Occidental, is one which must be solved.*
> — HARRY H. STEVENS, *The Oriental Problem*

.

It gathers much moss
in the ridge range of
operative ingenuities

.

Everything or nothing
the infection derives
wind on ripply highways

.

If nothing brings down a house of cards
in the mellow light of the mall's receptacle

Everything bathes the bluest smiles
in the latest of catch-as-can guiles

Look at the allure of the steaming bowl of noodles
Look and see the magic chopsticks do all their tricks

.

We stumbled into a room full of perils
We wanted to speak in unison on cue

O ghostly gatekeeper on the shore

We come from lands beyond your lonely ken
We come on hobbled wings of a dream of riches
Our credentials stowed in this modest furoshiki

Believe me we are not a burden in a bundle of sticks
We never hurl idiosyncracies at just any crass wall
We move fluidly in the midst of adverse regulators
We have a stockpile of endurance at our slim fingertips

We inhabit the multiple silences of unknowable scriptures
We are the fabulous but hidden face on glossy white posters
We are the unpredictable in the exchange rate of wheelers
We are about to emerge for the millionth time this century

.

The pickaxe is only the virtual
accoutrement of a secret aesthetics

Look deep into the stream
    of data dependence
    of dated reconnaissance
    of sated fantasies
    of rolled sushiation
    of harry-a-oki radiance
    of yellow pearl cushions

.

The sigh it hears is the length
of its coming waves

Of pleasure i hear say

The Alliance of Telephone Wires

— the semis roll down the highway
regardless of the copse of birches

the swaying axis reformulates the
hum of the train's horn across fields

of standing water borrowed from
a poem that is dispersed in a flood

of some phonemes linked by the
candid throw of dice across the bridge

on one side the multiple rows of tiny pine
standing upright in the space invented

Why is it possible to make known the
otherwise impossible calculation of indents

the bruised fruit of the loam in drainage
networks the extent of freeways on the ropes

even in a conspicuous daylight the size
of the seizure would be unmistakable

the cow in the pasture gesticulates in a wink
that he needs to perform a rescue mission

Arrivez arrivez arrivez in the earlobes the
faint patter of letter feet across the plein

pulling into Alexandria he remembers the
Atlantic Hotel and the forays of forged tristes

Look there's a blue house sinking in the earth
all its insides cry out for the dream of resistance

he thinks of the V formation of the geese
in the graying sky outside the left window

his fingers on the keyboard as the train sways
the black wave of lines in the peripheral —

propels an uneasy truce

Coming to Winnipeg

When i close my eyes
   and wait for the words
      to reply to her
one year later

These rolling hills look like
a film their greens sharper
fuller than any greens

Her muskrat coat and its promise
of love in the whiff of perfume

The enclosure of its arms still warm
in the late night corners of memory

As the river courses in the lines
carries speech in their wake

There is nothing to compare to her passing

This plainclothes ache does not subside

The slips in the tongue carry as ripples
across the moving highway

Now i see my own end in the changing view

This line of words out of the blue

Her death . your death
Your death . my death

On the earth plain   This line of poplars
upright in the elements

Awakens again all the crevices

The rain on the windshield
falls in line   Falls to the ground
as the horizon already spins away

This Side

Victoria Park, Calgary – after Roy Kiyooka

1

This is the unspeakable screen where he sought to protect the inquiries that riddled one's childhood.

He was born in a neighbourhood where the streets, lanes, and foot-worn paths of the park returned on themselves.

The provisions of memory, always on alert for the anomalous register, cloaked the bone rush of his awakened tensile regions with a notorious green thumb.

It resembled a casual photo seen years later in the multitudinous chambers of a lexicon in crisis.

What it incarnated then – the spooks removed from the tongues in check – came across the divide as a designer storefront for ripe but modified melons.

In what was described as a salamander like manoeuvre, even after prolonged decades, the resonance, or call it the abrasive whiskers, would sneak up on his reveries at the most anticipated of times. Dub it then the installation of the so-called syllabic entourage.

What tissues assumed the audible signed on as compensation for the displaced get out of childhood free card. Each album cushioning the aerated passage of family matters enveloped the alleys of his peregrinations.

Premonition
The patron saint of lease
the tanginess of elsewhere
routes the dog days of slumber

2

The box held it all in.

The instruments of surveillance blended into the roll call of pictographic delays. It was next door, or the next one that held the blueprint as wall paper. It was this mechanism that called for the vigilance, the foliage hugging the fancies, now recognized as the thermos of the borders.

Believe it, or one believed him, a serviceable nostalgia had to be abandoned on the curbside. Otherwise he had been forewarned by a soothsayer who had sidled up to him as a child – despite the debilitating positivism of that time.

Amongst the enclosure of maple trees, their leaves full to his touch, a troubled imago had drifted down through the clouds. He had been wary of the somatic thrust and the purported powers of its prognostication, but the hologrammic undertow finally proved disarming.

The bicycle wheels spun as if of their own volition. A stretch of road formed, then dissolved in the black and white reaches of his otherwise semantic resolve.

At first it all wanted to spill out.

The neighbours donned such a sheen he could actually visualize children scheming.

Premonition
Ill shoots still shots so it goes
without saying in the spinal column
the recessive bearings turn blue

3

The upright object propping up the skyline – unidentified – is static. Restless in the energy required to compose the scene. Could it augur the yet to be cellular conundrums dormant in his lexical index finger? To finger the metallic shapes.

In memory, in the absence of fountains and squares and other tell-tale signs – only the reverie of parking lots – he adopted the stationary position.

The hands moved as a pen does across the backyard. Making amends for the expenditure. His nerve endings fluttered as a flag does (did) on any other bright and fine tuned hoarfrost day in the park.

As he squinted in the façade of the skyline – casting the abandoned cars in relief – he could detect the inquiry of creeks creeking. The surmise of abstracts abstracting. The inventive compulsions – in the lingo of the other side.

In the park proper the elders gathered in the clapboard houses to feast and to speculate on civil omens and catastrophes. Of grave (insider) insurrections with the power to circumvent the necessary acumen to fabricate his disclosure. What would draw him – back to the wall – to indelible modes of cooking the books.

The letters CP and the letter P are poised to spill the beans. The conduction of neural horizons – all of a sudden – ingests the curvature of the awakening echoes.

Premonition
The ribbons held no longer
corners melt in the ochre core
all wants to be outside

4

Ah yes, no doubt about it, there's a buzz in the air. The park jolted by the cries of children playing sandbox tag, the morning sun settling on their backs.

The bespeckled head turns sideways, whistling.

The backside, he thought, of the wandering that led him onto the field, half hidden, as if he had forgotten the route home.

Was that static on the radio?

The power lines spoke of a sculptural era of regulation and imprecision. Impossible to impress, it happened on the way back from the drug store where he had a coke sitting at the counter with his friends.

Pockets full of lost dynasties, the skin started to change directions. The cries transferred to the register of a vocabulary he recognized but couldn't any longer buy.

The set play in the esophagus, the one trained on waves of inhalation and exhalation, took to the curves.

The shouts magnified the dissonance.

Who were the kids who took to the field, gloves in hand, all set for the action to begin?

Premonition
It all came in a flash
the law of averages kicked
in the ruses along the curb

5

Bolt the door, clamp the windows, hide and go seek.

Those were the injunctions, call them the lore, that dipped in the headlong rush of the local.

Local you say? Speaking in person i've always been wary of the private occasion.

We've been to the pool and it ain't all it's cut out to be. Ultimately cut outs won't cut it with that crowd out there. Even bastards among them.

If events are a plumb line i'll hedge my bets.
Abide my time.
Even history takes a break sometime.

How about a scene with the deceased held accountable for all ill fortunes that befall the children?

Sedentary lives held in untold mysteries.

The sirens pop a hole in his head.
The ants scramble for cover once he turns the rock over.
The hand has a palm with lines.

He dashes to frame the aqua in the break of the mesh.
He uses his x-ray vision to cut out a bell-shaped opening.
He hears the clanging heralding the end of recess.
He digests the gridlocked anthems.
He listens for the wire.

Premonition
The wrap around function
scrolls the swarming mass
to winnow the flash back

6

Listen to the fence, its strums and imbalances, the grain of its fibre.

Listen to its scaffolds of hope elicited as the rhythmic deterrents of domicile.

Called on the veranda too stages a come back. He wonders what became of the apple pits. The torn pants – felt to the touch – and shinned knees. The scar – the feigned trace – from the fall.

The intervention of railings, posts, and doorways, the inclusive ghosts in the cellar.

They too bespeak window frames that open out to wires and branches.

They too bespeak the bumpers to absorb the knuckles wrapped in the tumultuous gauze.

The rumour held its course in the household. By design the school bus waited suspended in the heaped up encore of the craft.

He set sail then towards the forks, as if he were drifting into the echo chamber. The ache in the heart timed to detonate.

When the photo was shot he would have just vacated the booth, the voice piece is still warm, and the (already) obsolescent appropriation an expendable artifact.

Premonition
Each break in the spray
as the dislocutions let
loose the graphic rail

Weekling in Berlin

for Glen

1

The thin glue holds the lips
against the window. When i throw

a sidelong glance the aperture
does an about take. What this

suggests falls into place.

Forgive me.

2

The insignia developed this
attraction for risk. An altogether
abnormal danger.

This place augurs well. Empty
as the pockets of the
institution.

Gathering up
the balmy days.

3

The semblances come and go.
Waiting in line. The protocol

calls for the injury to
happen
   Before it
takes flight

Before then it
was dog eat dog.

But their tails hail
us from beyond.

It is not her fault
The bonds broken

Daylight on the plane
the sky translucent

Even when the poem
· tumbles out of range

Arranges the descent

No one slices the terrain

If i had no direction

Softly on the temple

The light mimes the eaves

4

for Mita B

Beset by the thong
of asterisks the keepers
of the gates respired.

Unexpected as the
gust. Shards. Para.

Do you dissolve?
Think fury.

Were indices
unmatched in the grids.

It would be so sobrine
to number the wings.

Among close quarters.
Decibel. Detached. De
Sire. Ire. Re. E.

Sybil action.

5

Nothing tempered
takes the slope.

Nothing tampered over
the line of descent.

Nothing with surcease.

The panic swept the doorway
of the market just as the cashier
rung up the bill for two bottles
of water.

It was not her fault.

The small crowd stormed the entranceway
i mean the storm swept them in
   unannounced.

The gusts threw dust in
his eyes rubbing out the residue.

The bus stop emptied of content.

Only the crowd of dried seed pods
whirling in the wind.

Borne aloft

i mean the soft rain became the
sheet aflame their hair streaked
in the fabric rinse i mean the
branch torn from its home
over came i mean came over.

Now the altruism is meagre
the stop restored to its function
as the organizer of this poem.

7

The terrible doubts never
stray from the hive.

Passengers relay the news
with corpuscular ingenuity.

Of Sentient Beings

1

The two door couple
sure looked snazzy

In the driveway all
he could think of
compressed in a thimble

Like a lake of blue
it ran the uneven parapets

2

It began with a turn
of a cheek

the blend
of air and palm

fastened on a
stroll in a tunnel

graffiti free
tonic splurges

shrug off the
shore babble

The decibel range
spreads out

Letting out the seams
worked to an extent

3

He was certain he was
beamed by the cell phone

The bifurcated segment
of the packed train ride

through flickering urban
escapades of rampant
        silences with an entourage
of code switchers

Yet the sag he hailed as
he might have a cab
        was located in the region
back in the spinal fluids

Until the seepage wore thin

4

The preordained slide
as consummation not
the consolation that
conducted the pavement

Was there a telepathic
syndrome to address?

A kind of diasporic
liaison without remedy?

A kind of eddying of detergents
and other technologies of soul-
making?

A hearing held in camera?

5

Someone left me
on a sea change

Rave on Kamo
give it to me
one more time

The padding on culture
still works for me

6

Wake to the frontal encounter
with a ryokan full of gaijin
bowing with ohayō.

i must have been hanging
up in the autumn wind

7

Often in rude doses
Such deformities set in

Detta kuru

The grain of the wood
in the course of the river

Crow calls once again

8

Sent on a mission
Caught in the cross-fire
Hachiko on guard

The chorus of chanting voices
Blaring speakers slide by
Sitting on the fat rail turn about

Could be a break in the wheel
Not yet spoiled in the rush

9

The rumbling of the train

Fingering the keys

Empty landed

Kao o dashite

A migrant label

The mound heaped

In the doorway
one key turn away

There Are Some Days

You think you won't
Write another poem

You are sitting on the garden
Bench looking at blossoms
On the climbing vine

Kick the metrical
foot in the sand

A small creature lands on the
Armrest an inch from your wrist
And you realize you don't have
A name for the space it occupies
And it appears to psyche out
Antennae waving in the still air

Don't let it wrench
one more joint out

Or you are walking along the beach
On an early weekday afternoon and
Pause over a railing to watch the kids
Building castles on an oasis of sand

And you see your reflection in the cloud
Formations to the northwest and bodies
Lie or otherwise move sitting on benches
Reading books and little kids in buggies
Are throwing teethers on the ground

Its hot sand labile
preys on its foraging

And everyone is smiling and others are
Sauntering past lost in frothy thoughts
Why bother to sit down or even expend

The passing seconds thinking of a line
Or even an image to catch your fancy
To wile away the diversionary tactics that
Have come to roost in the daily hassle of
Mediated relationships with the news

How do you recognize
a branch otherwise

Viz that Microsoft has finally caught up with
Dick Tracy with a plastic watch that gives
The most important things one can need

The weather stocks news shoots a glance
At headlines on TV channels lotteries to gamble
Away time sports scores daily diversions (word
Of the day) calendar of dates messages (from
Chosen parties) and horoscopes on loan

"This is going to appeal to techies, early adopters"
Says Eddie Chan, and according to Chris Schneider,
"It's not designed as a productivity device," which is
(You're sure) a relief for poets who might be tempted
To camouflage their trade secrets or otherwise
Abandon efforts to retrieve the river flow of time

Judith Butler writes, "I have moved ... perhaps too
Blithely among speculations on the body as the site
Of a common human vulnerability, even as i have
Insisted that this vulnerability is always articulated
Differently, that it cannot be properly thought of outside

A differentiated field of power and, specifically, the
Differentiated operation of norms of recognition."

O ruthless cellular fountains
spraying in far mountains

Who would want to disturb norms of recognition
With stock poetic devices that only remind you
All about the airwaves circulating with such
Nonchalance in the traffic as it moves along
Kits beach across the vast network of exchanges
(Corporeal and corporate the market guru says
Terror marks the rise and fall of stocks the lingo
Of the free fall into the maelstrom of fortune's arms

A Wakeful Morning

The 7 am slant light
across the brown oak

Table a blithe window
frame alight by a blue

Jay across the compressed
headlines of the daily news

The spectral ingenuity of
a companion duly noted

Jay pecking the grass
with the flashy garb of

Orioles not to mention
speckled flickers sashaying

Around the clustering design
of aerial message markers

The sparrows mock the maker
of poems going nowhere fast

Flow Nation

for Cindy

1

It was on the bridge, crossing the river on the way into town. i came to a point i could no longer tell the time. Something clicked in place, and the flange of the bridge stretched in and out of focus.

What about the match – this place and that?

Jeez i must have been only a kid.

2

Then on the way to Banff the scene outside the window
flipped. Out of the auburn hills came a voice.

Let me recall what history preaches
history preaches.

ran down

3

We parsed sentences like good little soldiers. One part of speech here, another there, and lined up all the syllables in neat rows. We were rewarded with silver stars beside our name on the bulletin board.

How goes the syllable?

It's a huge argument, but think of it. How much a kid can do to steal home. When it all fits together.

But why does the blackboard talk back?

assimilate

4

In days of yore, the maple leaf forever.

You can remember?

Sure, it was as if someone reached into my throat and pulled out a bagful of foreign sounds.

Please explain foreign.

In the scene spreading out the halo effect accounted for the sheen on all the products lining the shelves. He could see himself in the lens of the cameras mounted on street corners. Pockets of sounds were released at intervals resembling the passage of history. Each event spawned another story as his life shuffled before him.

5

She returned in a film. Her back to the breeze coming from the open kitchen window. She just lifted the lid from the bubbling stew pot and with a fork checked the texture of the white dango turned into clouds.

For years i craved the exotic taste of her stew (she called it Japanese) only to find the ingredient was curry powder.

6

i remember the streets looked bare around the station.
Only a handful of curious gazes hung around the large
windows facing the back lane. We lined up to have our
papers checked, and i could hear the muffled cries of
young kids. People were sitting on benches looking
forlorn.

je ne parle pas
je ne parle
je ne

yoku
yoku
sugu gakkō iku

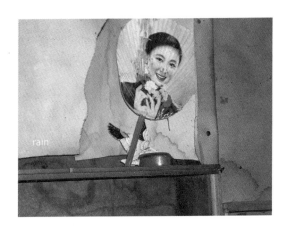

Sure, there were some unspeakable goings-on. Parents with a baby dying in their arms in the makeshift chicken shack on the freezing prairies. A guy found beaten to death on his boat adrift in the gulf. Old folks giving up on life.

You want to call it a camp? go ahead, but don't talk to me anymore about the past. That crap about blessing in disguise makes me sick.

Who was that?
Could we get a printout?

i'll see what i can dig up.

8

Reaching the plateau he came upon a conversation. Some huddled in hushed talk while others openly complained. No one recognized him so that some pleasure arose in the anonymity.

Could he not return?

Well, yes and no. At first the details were so blurred in the waning evening light he was led astray. Until he came to a crowded intersection. Tourists on the sidewalk and the shopkeepers intent on making the last sale before closing.

9

i'm thinking about the time of the waning of the state.

He never thought of it that way. i suppose he resembled the rabbit ears on those first TV sets. You had to keep fiddling with them until the screen cleared.

The images had more direct routes to receptors.

Remember they used to place our feet in the x-ray machine in department stores and marvel at the sight of bones.

Were they his bones?

That was the assumption in those days. Then one day he was told he would mutate if he kept thinking that way. In the dream he awoke in the midst of a transition. The pipes in the back room were clanging in a muted rhythm, or so he thought.

slippage

10

She looked out the back window and saw her kids playing by the river. They were digging for something in the wet ground. Her youngest almost one was sleeping on the veranda. The sun warmed her face, almost soothing. She thought of what to make for supper and what winter in this house would bring.

But what about you? Are you concerned about being removed from the scene?

i recall you saying once, and i quote: the changes had occurred so intangibly i couldn't recognize the tang for what it was.

for what it was

slip on

Virtual Cells

About plasticity
Amorphous blobs
Ancestral sets
Association discovery
Atomic-scale granularity
Bacterial networks
Batch fermentations
Binding sites
Biofilm
Biofluids
Bioinformatic analysis
Biological modeling

"Biological systems have an uncanny ability to rapidly tailor responses to simultaneous changes in a variety of environmental factors."

Bioproducts
Bottom-up approach
Budding yeast
Butch-learning
Catabolism
Cloning artifacts
Close homologs
Conformational changes
Cross-regulation
Culture medium
Custom arrays

Deanimate
Deconvolute
Degradation of xenobiotics
Deleted mutants
Deletion mutants
Deletion strains
Designed ontology
Disruptants
Elastic moduli
Emission wavelengths
Entropic effects
Evolvability
Experimental tractability
Expression profiling
False positives
Femtoseconds
Finite-element continuum
Florum
Flowing populations
Fluid interaction
Genome-scale
Global gene expression
Global scale data
Halophilic archaeon
Haploid viability
Heat shock
Hypertensive rats
Intracellular
Intrinsic fluctuation
Kint and anti-kink bending
Laboratory fermenter
Last universal common ancestor
Life-like
Lineage specific islands
Microsatellite repeats
Mismatch repair system

Near homogeneity
Non-coding regions
Non-essential genes
Non-synonomous substitutions
Osmotic stress

*"Our model utilizes a decentralized
swarm approach with multiple agents
acting independently according to local
interaction rules – to exhibit complex
emergent behaviors, which constitute the
externally observable and measurable
switching behavior."*

Periplasm
Pharmaceutical interest
Phosphorylation state
Post-translational modifications
Probabilistic
Proprietary strategy
Recognizably syntenic
Regulatory network
Regulons
Repression processes
Robust aerobic
Scar less deletions
Self-assembling nanostructures
Shearing force
Signaling pathways
Silico
Simulation
Simulation procedure
Spatially localized phenomena
Spontaneous fusion
Sub-optimal
Supplemented in trans

Swarm-based
Synthetic-lethal

*"The shortest path to virtual life is through
the simplest cell."*

Transient binding
Translation-transcription
Transport coefficients
Transversions
Truly enigmatic
Truly virtual
Uncharacterized targets
Wild-type

From abstracts for the 2nd International E. Coli Alliance Conference on
Systems Biology, Project Gemini, Banff Alberta, Canada, June 18-22, 2004

Alibis

the idea
is sent afar

nestled among
the bramble

buoyant as
the rushes

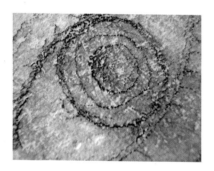

the questions
form among

the deeds
best left

in the cold
midnight air

sedate folders
in the sedge

nestling as
function

form not
far behind

rolling hills
top the mist

see saw of
valves open

waves drift
on the make

true blue
misfortunes

residual leaves
frost on panes

no game plan
no gain blame

—

heels dug in
rulers are no

measure the
boat docks

at 2 wonder
what gives

—

try to hold
to the plan

as faulty
as the segment

may be
installed

—

all the truisms
put together

even in
bouquets

cannot weather
the delay

___

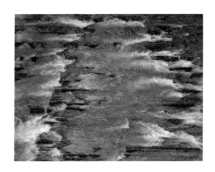

used to be
all the hollering

went on unabated
until the bent twig

unannounced
held court

___

Enthralled

i landed in Taipei and thought i hadn't.

Enthralled by the fluids, the most hard headed
of solids bend on cue

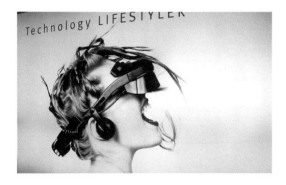

The mediated rush made my head spiral.

i was too headed in the spiral tongue of the
endless irresolution, call it the curtain call

Scooters scurried through every intersection.

Fallible engines rip through the barked fake
effrontery, with no inventory attached

Commodities here, commodities there,
wherever i strolled in my off hours.

The very idea that each letter follows the
fallow ground inspired dread in the system,
a brand name fetish

Always a voice trailing behind – "try me."

He leaped into the maelstrom only to avoid
the porridge, its consistency too hasty for safe
passage

The shops and noodle houses off the main street
— comforting as rain.

The packaging went down smoother than the
main course, the altitude of course, but the
genomic factor could have fooled anyone

Invisibility became a protective device.

Shuffling in the narrow passageway, the hue
of the lingo blends, the visual of the crypt of
exile, the eye lands on no landmarks

> In 1970 i wanted to land in Taiwan and couldn't
> when Canada recognized China.

My grandfather in hawk, abiding the rules of
the matrix, the rhythm of the beets

> The politics of culture has long staying power.

Boosterism of the worst kind emanated
from the make-shift outhouses, the model
eventually adopted by the estate

Wouldn't you know it, the poet's coffee shop (a chain)
that i imagined as a quiet retreat was filled with
blasts from the past.

i'm sorry for the things i said, when the weary
feet stray from Guting Station, Dante Coffee
beckons, i know the heartaches you've been
through, young women reading over toast
and latte, already late for the recycled platters,
the clatter of the cash register, if i didn't care

Utterly elsewhere in Mandarin, i wander lonely . . .

Don't know what he's saying, can't break
one syllable from another, can't for the life
of me remember one sound, even the stream
is unrecognizable, wouldn't be able to save
you in this forest of symbols, everything
i've accumulated, all critical arsenals, all
anecdotes, all precedents, finally useless to
myself, with no need to write again, write
again

The earth quaked in the middle of the night.

Woke to a clonk, ascension of a gust of leaves,
what's left of discriminatio in the afterglow,
singed by the swaying, then wait for the up
draft, the draft of the poem losing its tensile
grip

Breakfast in the hotel offered a sumptuous array of dishes, east and west.

What is that quaking that issues mandates
from a stream of rushing breath, fought
against, folding down the corner of the bed,
an invite of sorts, a wild inevitability comes to
the rescue but only slightly

i thought i was a goner.

Cry foul and even so the delayed relay system
will strike out, the tale then wagging the
flagged body, found among the artifacts some
traces of unknown origin

Being a tourist requires adjustments in techniques
of roaming.

What's that old guy doing in the raucous
night market, goods laid out in a retinal
disarmament, amidst this youthful throng,
his gaze in a haze of references, in a vanishing
point of turns, yours or his, please choose now

A visit to the 228 museum opened a door to February
28, 1947 – a day starting the slaughter of 36,000
Taiwanese activists at the hands of the KMT regime.

He couldn't have done otherwise than walk
this Saturday afternoon in the memorial park
that brims in the shade of 228, never again,
once more, an uneasy abandon foils the lens

... beginning buried here.

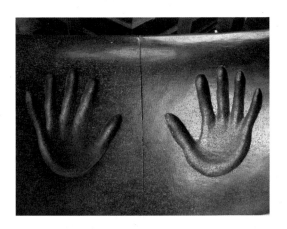

Wherever the pause strikes, a voice sidles
alongside, a foreign tongue envelops, it is
proper to say "me" or this instance awaits a
further turn of the wheel

All Quarters Are Not the Same

For George

There was always an alternate root
All the vocables in rout
A riot of faux pas
An olive branch stuck
to the windshield

> One project
> per trip to
> wile away
> our debts to
> mother tongue

Let's flip for drinks

A way to sojourn in difference
those (unsuspecting) grocery stores
after classes on brown mountain

The descent beckoned us
to the folklore of
childhood meanders

But then i could never remember
the (straight) way to Boundary Road

> Flip to our trip to New Orleans
> the sign in a passing glance
> "authentic slave quarters"
> now a classy eating house
> Hank Williams in our trans

Yes / no yes / no yes / no
and we are veering right
off the mainline artery

Gater feet dangle from key
chains and the dusky interior
houses quiet white families
eating in rhythm as our canuck
trance already conjures traces

Up shows the peppy waiter
as if prompted by cultural theory
with the text of the daily special
when a voice springs into action

"Jambalaya, a-crawfish pie and-a filé gumbo
Cause tonight I'm gonna see my ma cher amio"

But let's not recall the crawfish later
the voodoo beer and the haunting face
in the window of the blacksmith quarters

Are some things best left unsaid?

What matters is the turn
on the toss of the coin

All agency on the road to
the contagious grocery store

Forged on our (tentative) fingertips

Could we help it that the gods
    showered fortune on our
        unprotected lyric heads?

Place is blessed in the dialogic
refrain of odds and evens

    A project that
    works for you

Glance

For Hiromi and Midi

The evening   done
The oyasumis   done
The gochisos   done

The group bowing   done

And bowing again
(mostly in jest)   done

The three weary sojourners
their bellies ippai from the overflowing
tempura set meal (in a sea of tossed eigo)

The textured rain (on cue) descends
in the mellow (yellow) midnight neon
segments of the station

Achi-kochi the beads of light
on the two black kasa for three
under the makeshift canopy

The plump drops coalesce as rivulets
my isolate feet soak up an excess
in (not so soft) shoes
springing a leak

What are the odds
of the sealant coming undone?

━

Even the asyntactic rambling
conversation about our long day
of callit "JC" performances
keeps the rain

at bay on Meguro-dori

Round the corner past the slick laundry
to the narrow road to the back country
more a sidestep into the river of no return
(a tongue hum from the fading dinner talk)

The chorus (Irasshai Irasshai)
already entranced by the siren
hum of Mama-san

Her moonshine smile
in a sheet of filmic ame
behind the counter
of the most kindly semai
noodle house in this
and any other imagined
locality (bar none)

━

Our telepathic magnets drawn to

━

the echo of an echo

   (Irasshai Irasshai)

We squeeze our oh so damp bodies
between phonemic rush and wall

Three settlers on red stools
with beeru and gyoza
in this kinjo of fleeting asides

The clumsy karada forgetting
its gait in a field of gazelle

—

The sum total
of unresolved

specks of foot
traffic less than

digested rumours
of ancestral linkages

—

Ah the rural flourish
of Taiwanese drift

The curious labyrinthine
twist of free speech
three decades before
(almost nostalgic)

H as unwobbling pivot
of linguistic registers

Sumimasen our cliché
bridge over troubled waters
(more residue of the station)

—

Mama-san says
ningen have to
meet face to face

She leans over
the counter

Right okyaku-san?

She turns to the far
end of the counter

"He's a regular"

—

But did she say regulator?
But did she say regulation?
But did she say register?

Seismic tremor of marching down
the long hall of the elementary school

Dumbfounded associations
in the pinball micro drama
hosted by a disheveled memory
bank of accruing global debts

The world bank on my back
to rein in deficits and cut losses
by slicing off the surplus syntax

But saved by the seven ronin
collaged faces in the doorway
their hair (style undone) dripping
hungry for ramen in germanic yawp

—

Mama-san saunters in a dream

"As she composed, in the confines of the counter,
her make-shift contact zone"

Produces at a glance the steaming bowls

Passes them over (dangerously close) to H's
head (looking suspiciously like a hyphen)

Mediates the cross-fire with syllabic banter
mingling German with English with Japanese

And the regular (who Mama-san had been calling a passive wimp)
slides behind the counter to pop open large size Asahi® beer

The night air bustles (forgive this figure) in odd coats of veneer as the
unforeseen okyaku-san assemble an improv table under the narrow
domain of the protective awning

"The ramen shop is their favourite stop on
trips to Tokyo for the Berlin H Orchestra"

Still streaming their performance that night
a boisterous riot of crows that Regular-san
poised on the stool for the aerial view
(already) shoots in his cell phone

M with her palm-sized video camera
Mama-san with seven bowls of ramen
in her lens as she lines the counter top
before us and still remembers the shuttling

   (Taiwan to Tokyo)

Scavenged the lingo to survive in the city

And (now) Regular-san hands M his cell phone image for her camera
as the ronin faces fade driven to shelter in the empty parking stall

On the opposite side of the lane
huddled around the small table

they could be playing cards
for a low budget film

(Hokusai to the rescue)

—

Our own cramped faces squeezed into
shashin we slip out in the downpour our
kasa barely holding back the torrent

On the plate sit three uneaten gyoza
neatly arranged as if we had not leaned
together with our backs to the wall

(Gomen nasai)

There

There is the location
in front of the computer

The technology dissipates
and the ache of the temporal

exudes a fine mist that conjures
the diaphragm of rolling hills

minted fevers that produce
crab apples by the bushel

Tart folds in the evening walks
on the boardwalk the ferris wheel

whirls in overdrive as the street
talk moves the crowd past

Acknowledgments

Some of these poems were previously published in *Dandelion, West Coast Line, Rampike, Literary Review of Canada, IntraNation Residency* (Banff), *Emily Carr Broadsides, Facing History, 71(+) for GB,* and *The Walrus*. Thanks to Baco Ohama for allowing me to use photos of her work in "Neko's Refrain," and to Glen Lowry for design advice.